Also by Robert Westall
published by Catnip

A Time of Fire
The Wind Eye
The Making of Me: *A Writer's Childhood*

Christmas
Spirit

Christmas
Spirit

✦

Two stories

ROBERT WESTALL

Pictures by John Lawrence

Catnip

CATNIP BOOKS
Published by Catnip Publishing Ltd.
14 Greville Street
London EC1N 8SB

This edition published 2007
1 3 5 7 9 10 8 6 4 2

A CIP catalogue record for this book is available from
the British Library

ISBN 978-1-84647-037-0

Printed in Poland

www.catnippublishing.co.uk

Contents

The Christmas Cat

CHAPTER 1 A Cold Welcome   3

CHAPTER 2 A Pine Cone in the Ear   17

CHAPTER 3 Money Matters   34

CHAPTER 4 A Game of Spies   51

CHAPTER 5 Double Visions   67

CHAPTER 6 Merry Christmas   81

The Christmas Ghost

CHAPTER 1 Christmas Eve   93

CHAPTER 2 Otto's Kingdom   104

CHAPTER 3 The Lift   114

CHAPTER 4 Black Widows   125

CHAPTER 5 The Return   131

CHAPTER 6 Five Minutes to Midnight   139

The
Christmas
Cat

For Caroline Walker
of Stockton Heath

CHAPTER I

A Cold Welcome

Granddaughter, I was once as young as you. My legs were as long and thin and could run as fast. I could climb a wall better than any boy, even when there was broken glass on top. And my glory was my red hair, so long that I could sit on it.

That was the year 1934, my parents were abroad, and I spent Christmas with my Uncle Simon. My Uncle Simon was a vicar. Vicars then were not like vicars now. If you know any vicar now, he is probably a young man who dresses in ordinary clothes, and tries to make friends with everyone, even if he has a rather desperate smile and a rather uneasy laugh. Vicars are a threatened species now, and they know it. Soon, there may be hardly any vicars left, and some will be young women.

But vicars then . . . they had the *Power*. They dressed all in black, and people were rather afraid of them. I have seen a vicar empty a railway carriage, just by sitting in it. Just being there, they made people, ordinary people, mums and dads, aware of their *Sins*. They made them feel feeble and wicked and helpless. So people avoided them if they could.

I did not want to go to the vicarage for Christmas. I would rather have stayed on at school, with the headmistress, who was a good sort. But my father had written: 'You must go and stay with Uncle Simon. He has asked for you. Perhaps you will be able to cheer him up.'

I had doubts about cheering myself up. Uncle Simon had no wife and no children. The family said he had given himself to God. God did not seem to have made a good job of cheering Uncle Simon up. Uncle Simon always sent dark small miserable Christmas cards with *Holy People* on them, that wished you a 'Blessed and Peaceful Christmas-tide'. I much preferred Santa, grinning with a sackful of presents.

Still, off I had to go, with my whole school trunk, and a purseful of silver sixpences, to tip the railway porters.

All I knew about North Shields, when I arrived that Sunday, was that the people there made their living from fish, and I would have guessed as much as soon as I put my head out of the railway carriage. There was a mountain of kipper-boxes on the platform, and the smell of kippers would have knocked me flat, if the smell from a mountain of dried cod-boxes had not pushed me the other way. Outside, the cobbles of the taxi-rank were stuck all over with tiny silver scales, and the air was thick with the smell of fresh fish, frying fish, rotting fish, boiling fish and guano. Seagulls sat on every rooftop, nearly as big and arrogant as geese, and splattered the slates with their white droppings and filled the air with their raucous cries.

When I gave the taxi-man the address of the vicarage, he stopped being jolly and friendly, and went all quiet, as if I, too, was dressed all in black and had a huge Bible in my hand. We drove through the town. Every street-end gave us a view of the river with its mass of moored boats. The men and women looked strange to my southern eye; the men in huge caps and mufflers, the women in black shawls. There were shops, but most people seemed to be buying stuff off little flat barrows. There were no cars and lorries, but a lot of horses and carts, and the cobbled streets were thick with flattened masses of horse-dung, looking a bit like big round doormats.

'Here's the vicarage, hinny,' said the taxi-man, pulling up with a squeak and a jerk. I saw a great high, black brick wall, with broken glass set on top in concrete. Tall, shut green gates. And dark trees, massing their dull green heads over the wall, like a curious crowd.

'That's a shilling, hinny,' said the taxi-man, putting my trunk on to the pavement. Then he added, doubtfully, 'I hope you'll be all right,' and drove rapidly away.

I stared at the wall and gate aghast. It looked like the wall and gate of a prison, or at least a home for naughty children. The gate looked as if it was locked; but I managed to wrestle it open, and saw a short weedy drive leading up to a house that might have been pretty, except that the smoke and soot of the town had painted it black, too. I dragged my school trunk inside, and closed the gate and went and knocked on the door of the house. The knocker gave a terrible boom that seemed to echo in every room inside. It seemed to make a noise that was far too important for *me*.

At last, the door opened. The woman who opened it didn't see me at first; she was looking over my head.

Then she looked down and saw me and said, 'The vicar's out.'

'But,' I said.

'But nothing. The vicar's out. He's down at the church if you want him. Saying Evensong. I've nothing for you here.'

'But . . .' I said again.

She'd closed the door in my face.

By this time, I was close to tears but I'd long since learnt that tears don't get you anywhere. So I sniffed them back, and went to look for the church

There were plenty of people around, but I didn't know who to ask. They were such a strange crew; Blacks and Chinese with pigtails, even the men. Groups who looked like Indians, only they wore rags round their necks and suits of thin blue washed-out cotton, and talked at a great rate in their own language. Men who might have been Spaniards, with gold earrings and thin moustaches and flashing smiles; and men who might have been Germans, with cropped hair, and a stolid unsmiling way of stumping along. Even the women talked in a strange accent, though you could pick out the odd English word.

Then I saw this ordinary man ambling towards me. He seemed to be slightly ill, for he swayed as he walked, and wobbled across the pavement, several times nearly falling into the gutter. But he had a nice face, and was smiling to himself. An unbuttoned sort of man; an unbuttoned overcoat over an unbuttoned coat, over an unbuttoned waistcoat.

'Please could you tell me the way to the church?'

He looked at me like a wise owl, and the smell of his breath was worse than the fish. Whisky. I always hated the smell of whisky. My father sometimes drank it, in the evenings, and I would not kiss him then.

'Aye,' he said, 'but which church? Are you a damned Papist, or a damned Nonconformist, or a True Believer?'

'Sir,' I said, looking him straight in the eye, so that I made him sway a good deal more. 'I am a True Believer!'

'God bless you, hinny,' he said, tears springing into his watery blue eyes. 'Ah'm a Sinner, a Terrible Sinner. It's the drink, you see. Ah drink and then Ah do terrible wicked things . . .'

'The church,' I said, as firmly as possible.

'Ah'll show ye.' And the next second, he had enclosed my hand in his huge warm dry one, and was leading me a staggering dance along the pavement, still telling me of his wicked sins, though not in any detail, which might have been interesting . . .

'There's the True Church,' he said at last, pointing.

And I had no doubt it was. For it was as black as coal, and the door was barred by huge rusty iron railings, and a black notice board announced Uncle Simon's name in small gold Gothic letters.

I thanked him; but he would not let go of me; he kept on going on about his sins. At last, I had a brain-wave.

'Come and see the vicar. He's inside. He's my uncle. He'll help you with your sins.'

'God forbid,' said the man fervently. 'My sins are
too black for any vicar to help.' And the next second,
he was gone.

The rusty gate was not so fortress-like as it looked.
It opened under my hand. So did the great studded

door. I was in dimness, with the saints staring down at me, all purple and red and blue, from out of their stained-glass windows. There was a smell of polish and Brasso and incense and dust and mice.

And the sound of my uncle singing. He had a very beautiful voice; his voice was the only beautiful part of him. He was singing half the service, and a cracked old voice was singing the other half.

'O Lord, open Thou our lips.'

'And our mouths shall shew forth Thy praise.'

'O God, make speed to save us.'

'O Lord, make haste to help us.'

I sat, and listened to the end. I listened to that lovely voice preach about the feeding of the Five Thousand. He preached very well.

The only thing was, that apart from me and the old lady at the organ, the huge church was completely empty.

'You walked down here by *yourself?*' said my uncle. 'You must never do that again. I cannot imagine what Mrs Brindley was thinking of, letting you come down here by *yourself.*'

He did not look at me. He looked at his pulpit, at the board that gave the numbers of the hymns, at the saints in the stained glass windows. Never at me. Not all the time I stayed with him. I got the feeling, in the end, that I was accompanied by an invisible person, two feet to my left, that my uncle talked to all the time.

'Why not?' I asked, greatly daring.

'Child! This town is filled with such wickedness that your poor young mind could not contain it. You cannot breathe the air of these streets without being defiled. Such *sins* . . .'

But he didn't go into any detail, which might have been interesting. Just like the poor whisky-man . . . My mind went over the wickedest things I knew. Which were not very wicked in those days, granddaughter. I have learnt a lot since.

'We must rescue your trunk. Before they steal it.' That at least made sense. We'd had thieves at school.

Together we hurried up the road. A way cleared before us, through the milling crowd, as if by magic. A lot of people actually crossed the road to avoid us.

My uncle seemed surprised to find my trunk still lying where I had left it. He picked it up with a grunt that made me worry for him. He was older, much older, than my father. He had silver hair; and an old cracked broad leather belt, round his long black cassock, that strained at the last hole. Tall and portly, my uncle was.

Mrs Brindley opened the door to his knock, undoing both the top and bottom bolts with a rusty squawk.

'Oh, it's you, Vicar! Is this young woman pestering you?'

'Of-course-not,' gasped my uncle, lifting my trunk again. 'She-is-my-niece-my-brother's-daughter-that-I-told-you-of.'

'Oh,' Mrs Brindley looked at me; for the first time, really. There was a certain amount of curiosity mixed with her hostility.

'Well, I only hope she's not too much for you, Vicar. You've got so much to do, and so have I.'

Such was my welcome at the Vicarage.

CHAPTER 2

A Pine Cone in the Ear

I spent three days of sheer misery. It was not that my Uncle Simon was at all a cruel man. He simply forgot I existed, unless I reminded him, and then he did not know what to say to me, and there were long terrible silences, especially at mealtimes.

I certainly wasn't starved. Meals were the one way Mrs Brindley spoiled him, and he ate a lot, and I ate a lot, too. It helped to fill up the silences at mealtimes. Real heavy stodge it was; worse than school.

But I was so *cold*. The vicarage was huge; like a great polished refrigerator of dark wood. My uncle had a fire in his study during the day; but I was forbidden to go there, in case I disturbed his reading. The only other warm room in the house was the kitchen, and that was Mrs Brindley's lair, and she hated me. She thought she owned my uncle, and I think she saw me as a rival.

I couldn't even stay in bed to keep warm; I tried that once, and Mrs Brindley soon rooted me out. Staying in bed during the day was sinful, and she had a terrible nose for sinfulness, like a bloodhound.

No, I must go out and play. Only when I went outside could I wear my coat and beret and scarf and gloves. Wearing them indoors was also sinful for some reason.

So I went out. Not, of course, out of the green gate into the sinful town. I soon learnt that Mrs Brindley kept a keen eye on the gate; I was even accused of going too near it, of *thinking* about going through it. No, I was confined to an acre of woodland, inside the high wall.

Woodland? It was ornamental trees of the darkest, most hideous sort. Pines and firs and monkey puzzle trees and holly bushes grown five metres high, with nothing but pine needles in between. And wretched dark rhododendrons. It couldn't even boast a bird, let alone a squirrel.

There were the old stables; they gave me a happy hour, exploring, for they had only just been aban-

doned. Harness still hung in the harness-room; there
was still staw and hay in the stalls, and even a pony-
cart with its spokes loose with damp and its tyres red
with rust. I thought of lighting a fire in the little grate
in the harness-room; but I knew Mrs Brindley would
soon spot the smoke from the chimney.

But it was there that I made my first friend. An old black and white cat with long thin legs and a bulging belly. She was terrified of me at first; but I had patience, and all the time in the world. And she was hungry, so hungry, and I got into the habit of smuggling an old cloth pouch into the dining-room, in the pocket of my cardigan, and popping titbits from my plate into it. My uncle never noticed; most of the time he was lost in his book at table; though my parents had always said reading at table was very rude. But I had to be careful when Mrs Brindley was about. Still, it was my first defiance, and my first victory.

My second victory started like a defeat. I was wandering aimlessly through the wood, by the high wall at the back, when a pine cone hit me sharply on the nose. It really stung; my eyes filled with tears. When I had wiped them, I stared around, but there was nobody about. I thought perhaps the pine cone had fallen off a tree; but as I was thinking that, another hit me on the ear.

I whirled round; no way had that one fallen off a tree. Again, there was no one to be seen. But I noticed one place where a dense holly tree grew up against the wall. It was the only spot in that dreary place where anyone could hide. I went on as if aimlessly wandering; but now I picked up the odd pine cone as I went,

choosing the wettest and heaviest ones and pretend-
ing to examine them with interest.

When I had about ten in the pocket of my coat, I
heard a third missile land in the pine needles behind

me. I spun quick as a flash, and saw the holly tree move, and threw my heaviest cone as hard as I could. Then another, and another. I was no mean shot at throwing a cricket ball, and now I could see a vague shadow through the dense leaves. My fourth pine cone hit the shadow. The shadow said 'Ow' in a loud voice.

My fifth cone hit as well; and my seventh. There was a frantic scraping of feet on the wall-top; then a smashing and crashing that carried on all down the tree. Something hunched-up landed at the bottom, on the dead dry holly leaves.

It was a boy, about eleven, my own age. He hugged himself and glared up at me.

'You silly tart! You've broke my leg.'

'You started it!'

'I didn't break *your* leg.'

'Let's have a look at it.' I started forward, a bit worried.

'Gerroff me.' He jumped up so quickly I knew his leg wasn't broken, though he was limping quite badly. He walked up and down, like a footballer who's been hurt, trying to walk the pain away.

'I can't climb the wall like this,' he stormed.

'Then you can go out of the gate . . .' I was glad he wasn't badly hurt.

A look of terror came across his face. 'The vicar

will catch me. He'll fetch the poliss to me. For trespassin'.'

'I'll say you're with me.'

'You're trespassin' an' all.'

'No, I'm not. I'm the vicar's niece.'

He eyed me with fresh horror, and turned and made a frantic attempt to climb up between the tree and the wall. But three feet up he stopped, grimacing with pain.

'I'll give you a leg-up if you like,' I said. And went and pushed up on his bottom until, with a terrible struggle, he made the top of the wall. 'Can you manage now?'

'I can drop down. I can crawl home. You can crawl even with a broken leg,' he said bitterly.

Suddenly I didn't want him to go. So, greatly daring, I said, 'I'm not Frankenstein, you know.'

'No,' he said. 'You just look like him.'

I got one of my last pine cones out of my pocket . . .

'O.K.,' he said, putting his hands in the air, like somebody in a cowboy movie. 'I surrender.' He grinned. He had rather a nice grin. It went with his snub nose. And his blue eyes were suddenly merry. 'You're not Frankenstein. Frankenstein wouldn't dare push a boy up the bum.'

'I'll come up,' I said. Anything he could do, I could do.

'Mind the broken glass,' he said. He had put his overcoat over the glass on top of the wall, and he moved along to make a space for me, and pulled up his long stockings that had fallen round his ankles, and wriggled himself inside his short trousers.

'I don't usually talk to girls.'

'Why not?'

'Girls are soft.'

'I'm not.'

'You're not a bad climber. For a girl. And a toff,' he said grudgingly.

'Who're you calling a toff?'

'You. You sit all lah-di-dah in that big vicarage and eat banquets off silver plates. All toffs do. And ride round in big cars and tread on the faces of the workers.'

I'm afraid I burst out laughing. Though it was a cold little laugh.

'You'll not laugh when the Red Revolution comes,' he said fiercely. 'We'll string your sort up from lamp posts.'

'*You'd* do that to *me*?'

He gave another grin, with a bit of shame in it. 'Well, not you personally. But the vicar ... Religion is the opium of the masses.'

'Who says so?'

'My Uncle Henry. He's only a labourer, but he's read Karl Marx.'

'If you only knew,' I said, 'how us toffs really live.' And I told him about being so cold all the time.

'By heck,' he said, 'you ought to come to live wi' us workers. Me granda's a retired miner. We're not short of coal. Every time I go to me Nana's I break out into a sweat. Specially today. It's her baking-day. Hey,' he turned to me, 'why don't you come? It's only across the road . . .'

I looked down the other side into a back lane with cricket wickets chalked on the brick walls, every ten yards or so. It didn't seem too hard a drop. I glanced at the gold-plated watch that my father had given me for my last birthday. It was two whole hours until Mrs Brindley would call me for tea. I looked up and caught him looking at my watch, and thinking I was a toff again.

'S'all right. We won't nick your watch. When the Revolution comes, we'll *nationalise* it. All proper and legal . . .'

'Thanks,' I said. 'That's a relief . . .'

'Us workers is honest. Not like the thieving bosses, grinding the faces of the poor.'

'Shut up,' I said. 'Or I'll grind your face personally.'

'You don't talk like a girl at all.'

I think he meant it as a compliment.

We walked up the back lane, past women who were gossiping by their gates, their arms entangled with their black shawls. They had very lined faces, and gaps in their teeth as they grinned.

'You courting, young Bobbie?'

'Hallo, hallo, who's your lady-friend?'

Bobbie muttered darkly under his breath. I thought for a moment he was going to take to his heels, and leave me standing there. But he went up to a back gate and opened it, saying:

'This is me Nana's.'

The yard was full of washing, billowing sheets pegged carefully in position so that their snowy white bellies missed touching the sooty brickwork by a fraction of an inch. I edged through them, gingerly; they reached out and enfolded me like clammy ghosts. I was lost in a wilderness of snowy wetness . . .

'Don't touch them,' came Bobbie's muffled voice. 'Your hands'll make them dirty, so she'll have to do them again. Just keep walking.'

I emerged damply from my shroud at last.

'She takes in washing,' said Bobbie, his voice a bit subdued. 'From the toffs. Retired miners don't get much; you have to make ends meet.'

He opened the back door and yelled, 'Yoohoo.'

A yoohoo in reply came from the right. He opened the door and a blast of heat, like a furnace-door being opened, hit me.

The room was lit with a red glow, in which a lot of bits of brass glinted like red jewels. Horse-brasses

hung round the kitchen range; little rows of miniature pots and pans and windmills on the mantelpiece.

There were great bowls of dough, set to rise in front of the range. Half the great table was covered with wire racks of cooling bread, of all shapes and sizes. The smell was wonderful.

And on the other half of the table, his Nana was kneading dough. Great muscular arms rising and fall-

ing, large hands twisting. She had a powerful beak of a nose, and her dark hair pulled back in a tight bun, and little patches of flour on her high forehead. She gave me a quick look, her hands never stopping. Her small dark eyes missed nothing about my clothes, my watch, the way I stood.

She knew I was a gentry-child, as I knew from the straight-backed way she stood that she had once been a cook in a big house, with a lot of kitchen-maids under her. But she didn't bat an eyelid.

'Won't you sit down, Miss,' she said, very stately and dignified as our cook might have said it. And gave me a wink.

'I'm afraid I'm not one of the workers,' I said. 'I'm just hanging on until the Red Revolution ...'

She threw back her head and laughed a great laugh. She still had all her own teeth. 'Our Bobbie's got a head full o' rubbish. Our Henry's always filling him wi' daft ideas. Give your guest a plate, our Bobbie. One of the best, the rosebud ones out o' the front room. You'll have a hot bun and butter, Miss, on a cold afternoon like this?'

I sat on her black horsehair sofa and ate a bun, two buns, three buns, dripping with melting butter.

'Set you up,' she said, thumping dough into loaf-shapes, 'for when those Red Revolutionaries come to chop your head off. Are you staying somewhere local?'

'The vicarage,' I said, expecting the Ice Age to descend at any moment.

But she just paused and sighed, and said, 'Oh, that poor man.'

It was the first kind word I'd heard about my uncle. I was so grateful I could have wept. She didn't miss that, either.

'It's that Polly Brindley,' she said, thumping the dough as viciously as she might have pummelled that lady. 'It's that Polly Brindley I blame. He was a canny little feller, your uncle, when he first came. Always gave you a smile. Till Polly Brindley got her claws into him. Like she got her claws into the last vicar. She thinks she runs the parish. Always coming to the vicarage front door and telling folks that the vicar isn't in, when he is. Or the vicar's too busy to bother wi' the likes of us. She's set people against him something cruel. And Ah reckon she's on the fiddle at the corner shop. She buys far more stuff than one poor man could ever eat . . . still, that's none o' my business. Another bun, Miss?'

She went on talking as she worked, and worked prodigiously. About the old days in the servants' hall, and the hunt gathering in the park for a stirrup-cup on New Year's morning. I think she told me things she hadn't thought about for thirty years. The time just flew, and our Bobbie listened open-mouthed. It must have been hard for a young Red Revolutionary to take. Then I looked at my watch. It was five minutes to tea-time.

'I must get back,' I said in a panic. 'Thank you for the buns.'

She smiled, a slightly sad smile. 'It's been nice talkin'. Come whenever you like. When you can get. She'll have you cooped up an' all, has she? No going out round the town, mixing wi' the riff-raff?'

'How did you know that?'

'I know my Polly Brindley. I was at school wi' her. She thought she was too good to mix wi' the likes of us, even in those days.'

Bobbie opened the door, and we went into the icy hall. As we stood on the worn doormat, I heard the sound of a racking cough upstairs. Terrible coughing, as if someone was coughing their very soul out.

'Me Granda,' said Bobbie. 'It's the coaldust on his lungs. She has him to see to, an all.'

Then we were running down the lane, to the high wall of the vicarage. Bobbie showed me where to put my feet, where two missing half-bricks made good footholds, and gave me a push on my bum in his turn. I threw down his overcoat, and then we heard the cold hating voice of Polly Brindley calling me from the kitchen door.

'Miss Caroline. Miss *Caroline*.' It wasn't the first time she'd called. She was brewing-up for making a fuss.

'Goodbye,' I whispered. 'Come again.'

'We'll string *her* up from the lamp-post,' he said,

'when the Revolution comes.'

I went back into that cold, cold house.

'You were a long time coming,' said Polly Brindley accusingly.

'I had to tie my shoelaces,' I said.

She sniffed her disbelief.

CHAPTER 3

Money Matters

Next morning, over breakfast, Uncle Simon looked up from the dark grey book he was reading. 'Only a week until Christmas,' he said, with a weak attempt at a smile. 'I've been thinking about Christmas. What we should do, now you've come to spend it with us. I thought of having a Christmas tree. But Mrs Brindley has pointed out that they are heathen things, Christmas trees, and she's quite right. Heathen things from Germany, worshipping Odin. Brought over by the late Prince Consort. Quite wrong in a vicarage. And their pine needles do make a mess.' He shuddered delicately, and I knew then that he was afraid of her. 'Still, we must get you some presents. But I'm leaving that to the good offices of Mrs Brindley. I'm sure I don't know what young ladies like for Christmas.'

And he returned to his book, and Christmas seemed already over, shot on the wing before it got to us, like a poor pheasant.

I felt so sick of Mrs Brindley, who came in at that moment to clear the table, and whom I was sure had been eavesdropping at the door, that I grabbed my coat and gloves and went out into the garden, where I could rage in peace.

A pine cone hit me on the ear.

'Don't start *that* again,' I said dangerously.

'Ey,' he said. 'Look what I got for you.' Dangling down the wall, I saw the rustiest old paraffin-stove I had ever seen in my life. The tall cylindrical sort, with three legs.

'We're not a *rubbish*-tip.'

'It works. My dad got it off the tip and mended it. You can have it in the harnessroom, to keep you warm. Make a den. Old Brindley will never spot this.'

'Mrs Brindley to you.'

'Us workers call her old Brindlebags.'

I couldn't suppress a snigger. He was awful.

'Only,' he said, 'it hasn't got no paraffin in it.'

'Well, what good is it?'

'I thought you might have some money . . .' he said

longingly.

'How much do you want?'

'Just tuppence. I've got a beer-bottle to carry the paraffin in!'

I reached up and gave it to him, and he vanished.

We sat on old wooden chairs, and stretched out our feet to the stove, which burnt well, in spite of the cracked glass in its window.

'We could brew tea,' he said. 'If we had some tea. Or roast chestnuts, if we had some chestnuts.' He sounded wistful. I couldn't help noticing how thin his legs were. And his shirt collar, though clean, was ragged.

'What does your father do?' I asked.

He said, proudly, 'He's a fitter, a foreman-fitter. He used to build ships. But they don't build ships any more. He's on the dole. But he can do all kinds of things. He can sole and heel shoes and mend bikes and sometimes a car for one of the toffs. We keep going somehow.'

'That's *awful*,' I said.

'Oh, we're lucky. My mam and dad have only got me; some fellers on the dole have eight or ten kids. They run about in bare feet, even in winter, 'cos they haven't got no shoes. Everybody's on the dole. But

they say, if a war comes . . . there'll be work for everybody again.'

'How awful . . . I don't want there to be a war.'

'A lot of my dad's mates would rather get killed
than rot on street corners. That's why there might be
a revolution . . .'

'Oh, don't start that again.'

Just at that moment, the cat walked in for her
morning scraps. She came as regular as clockwork,
now, though Bobbie had never seen her before.

'That's another poor bugger in trouble,' he said gloomily.

'In trouble?'

'Goin' to have kittens. Any minute now. Don't they teach you nothin' at your public school?'

'We only have dogs,' I said, a bit snootily.

'For chasing poor bloody foxes with . . .'

But I didn't rise to his bait. I was too worried about the cat.

'She can't have kittens here. It's too cold.'

'Reckon she hasn't got anywhere else to go. She's flipping starving.'

'But why hasn't she got a home? She's so tame.' The cat finished her bacon rind and came and rubbed against my hand for more.

'People chuck them out, 'cos they can't afford to feed them. Lot of people drown them. Put them in a sack and chuck them in the river. River's full of 'em.'

The cat rubbed against my hand, and looked at me, trusting, confiding.

And suddenly it wasn't a matter of kindness to animals any more; it was a matter of life and death. She was just as much in need of love as our dogs at home.

'This is *intolerable*,' I stormed.

'Ye'll just have to learn that's the way things are

round here. We have to put up wi' it. There's little bairns starvin', let alone cats.

'We must do *something*. Can't *you* take her home?'

'We gotta dog already, an' we can hardly feed that. Only the butcher gives me mam free bones, and she boils them for soup, then the dog has them afterwards.'

'What about your Nana?' I thought of that stout determined redoubtable woman.

'She's got two cats already. She couldn't cope with six more.'

'*Six?*'

'The kittens, stupid. Kittens grow up to be cats.'

'I could give her money for them . . .'

He gave a look that was suddenly cold, remote. 'We divven't accept charity.'

'Sorry,' I said. 'It's just that I'm scared Mrs Brindley will find out . . . she'd have them destroyed. She can twist my uncle round her little finger.'

'Aye,' he said bitterly. 'Reckon she'd have poor people destroyed if she could. When the Revolution . . .'

'Shut *up!*'

There was a long silence. After a while he said, 'I could build her a hiding-place. To have the kittens in.'

He got up, and rooted around the harness-room.

Got an old thick cardboard box, that said 'Nestlé's Milk, One Gross'. He went out to the stable, and came back with it half-full of clean crumpled hay. Then he folded the lid cleverly, leaving only a small hole in the top. Put it back against the wall, under the big table one used for cleaning harness. Laid one or two old planks of wood and an empty paint-tin on top.

His hands were clever. It was a good hiding-place, warm and dark, and no one would ever think of looking inside it, it looked so normal, boring. He gently picked the cat up and showed the box to her, let her sniff it. Then popped her inside. We listened to her rustling about in the hay, pounding it with her paws.

Then she poked her head up through the hole, and sat looking at us with such a comical expression of triumph on her face.

'She's tekken to it,' he said, in a voice of low glad glee. 'She'll have her kittens in there now.'

'If only the kittens don't cry out!'

'They'll knaa enough to keep their mouths shut, when the Brindley's prowling round.'

'You make her sound like a tiger or a wolf or something!'

'Aye,' he said grimly.

'There's one more thing worrying me. I'm stealing scraps from the table to feed her. If Mrs Brindley catches me . . .'

'Goodbye scraps. And goodbye cat . . .'

'Oh, don't worry,' I said loftily. 'I can tell a lie. I can lie as well as anybody when I want to. She won't find out about the cat. But I won't be able to come here any more — she'll be watching me like a hawk. Will you go on feeding the cat?'

'What with?' He shrugged, looking down at his feet, ashamed of his poverty and helplessness. 'She can't eat grass, you knaa.'

'I'll give you money to buy things. I've got plenty of money.' I reached into my purse and pulled out the five pound note that Daddy had sent me for the Christmas holidays. They were huge plain white things in those days.

'What the hell's that?' he asked. 'Your school report?'

'Five pound note.'

He took it from me and examined it closely; crinkled it between his fingers, smelt it, like a little animal. Then he gave it back quickly. The shine went out of his eyes; they went as dull as ditchwater.

'If the feller at the corner shop saw me wi' a *ten-shilling* note, he'd send for the poliss.'

'But it's all I've got,' I said, tears of frustration seeping into the corners of my eyes. 'Except two sixpences.'

'Ah can do a lot wi' a sixpence ...'

'No,' I said. 'I'll go to the bank and change it. What kind of money do you need?'

'Nothing bigger than a two-shilling bit,' he said.

'We'd better go now,' I said. 'Before it gets dark. It's an hour till tea-time yet.'

'C'mon then. Ah'll show you the sights o' Shields. Bring on the dancing girls ...'

You cannot imagine, granddaughter, the sights I saw that day. Groups of unemployed men, squatting at the street corners, passing round the flattened dog-end of a cigarette from one to the other; smoking it, with the aid of a pin stuck through it until it was only a quarter inch-long. A man with no legs, just flat worn black leather pads where his legs should be, singing carols in a deep sweet voice from a doorstep, with his

little dog nearby and a flat cap into which some passers-by put halfpennies.

But in the end we reached the bank, with its tall sandstone columns.

'You're never going in *there*,' whispered Bobbie, awe-struck.

'Why not?' I said. 'It's *my* money.'

And I sailed in, as I often had before, and the man behind the counter not only changed the note exactly as I asked, but called me 'Madam' of course. What was the difference between me and Bobbie, I wondered? I wasn't dressed grandly, I can tell you. Only a sensible country tweed coat and hat. But I suppose my voice was what Bobbie would have called posh. And the man behind the counter was my servant; I expected him to obey, and he did. With a little subservient smirk. I had a brief thought about Bobbie and his Red Revolution . . . were Red Revolutions infectious? The man behind the counter wouldn't like a Red Revolution at all. The workers would probably string him up from the nearest lamp-post. Before helping themselves to his bank . . .

When I got outside, Bobbie caught my arm.

'We'll have to run like hell,' he said.

'Why, for heavens sake?'

'It's starting to rain . . . Brindley'll be out in the

garden looking for you in a minute.'

I have never run so fast in my life.

Bobbie gave me a last heave up on to the wall, and I listened in the growing dusk. The vicarage lights were on, and the rain was now falling steadily.

'You got that money safe?' I whispered down to him.

'Yeah,' he whispered back. 'Best of British luck wi' Brindley.'

Then I was dropping down into the wet garden, and he was gone. I felt very alone. But rather excited. Like a spy. I listened more carefully. No sound of Brindlebags calling for me; that was bad. That meant she'd been calling and given up. Maybe she had even searched the garden for me, and not found me. Still, I walked round to the front door, sauntering along as if I didn't have a care in the world. As luck would have it, I met my uncle as he came through the gate.

'Caroline,' he said, 'what are you doing out in this rain?'

'Oh,' I said gaily, 'I sheltered in the old hayloft. It's quite dry up there.' How easy it is, to lie.

'I hope you looked where you were going,' he said. 'They say the hayloft floor is rotten in places . . .'

Just then, Mrs Brindley opened the front door.

'Where have you been, you wicked girl! I've looked everywhere for you. You were nowhere to be found ...'

I remembered the bank, where the man had been my servant. Mrs Brindley was also a servant, though she had long since forgotten her place.

'Oh,' I said, in a voice of disgust, 'I heard you calling. I'm sick of you calling for me. Like I was a pet dog. Or a cow.'

'Caroline!' said my uncle, in a very shocked voice.

Adamsons are *never* rude to their servants. It might have gone hard with me; if Mrs Brindley hadn't forgotten herself again, and been ruder back.

'She's lying. I looked everywhere.'

'Up in the hayloft?' I asked sweetly, looking up and down her massive fat body. 'How many rungs are missing on the ladder?'

She knew she was beaten there; she shot me a look of pure hatred. But she wouldn't give up. She turned to my uncle. 'She's so disobedient. I can't be expected to take responsibility . . .'

'I can be responsible for myself,' I said stoutly. 'I am nearly twelve years old . . .'

For the first time, I saw a flicker of fear in her piggy little eyes.

'Come, come now,' said my poor uncle, all atremble, 'let us have peace and harmony. This is a Christian household. I want a word with you in my study, Caroline.'

Mrs Brindley smirked and left, quite sure she had won. I followed my uncle into his cold study, with its poor, smoking fire. How different from Bobbie's Nana's generous blaze. And the hearth hadn't been swept properly. There was a rim of ash half-hidden behind the fender, half-an-inch high. Mrs Brindley was a slut into the bargain.

My uncle sat down, his pale podgy hands clasped between his black thighs.

'Caroline,' he said, as severely as he could muster, 'you know what I am going to say to you ...'

'She called me a liar,' I said coldly. 'She is a servant, and she called me a liar. What do you think my father is going to say about *that*?'

Poor weak man, how we tormented him, Mrs Brindley and I between us. He wrung his hands, and did not know what to say.

Except, 'Is there no peace in this world?'

I wondered then what God thought of me; for God was very close and real to me in those days. And then I thought of God's cat, God's creature that Mrs Brindley would destroy if she could.

'She is over-familiar,' I said. 'She has got above herself.' I thought of all the other things I might have said; the grocer's bin, the filthy fireplace. But I was only a child; he would not have taken it from me.

'She has so much to do,' he said. 'It makes her over-hasty. But she means it for the best.' Poor fool. I made up my mind then that I would destroy Mrs Brindley. But I just said, 'Very well, uncle. I will try to be civil to her,' and got up and went to the door.

'There was one more thing,' he said, with a little shy, timid smile, staring at something over my shoulder. 'Miss Stevenson — my organist — has sent to say she is unwell and unable to play for daily evensong. I was wondering if you would come and sing it with me?'

'With all my heart,' I said, and meant it. It was a way of saying sorry to God.

CHAPTER 4

A Game of Spies

He lifted the heavy latch, and the metallic clink echoed up and down the dark empty church. The stained-
glass angels of the windows were pointed islands of
dim light in the blackness.

'Wait here,' said my uncle, 'while I put on the lights.'
He walked into the darkness ahead, where only a tiny
red flame flickered high up in the sanctuary lamp; red
as blood. His footsteps were sure and confident, as if
he knew the way by heart.

Then the chancel lights came on, dimly golden,
and he was taking off his dark overcoat, and slipping
on his white surplice.

'You know the service?'

'We sing it every Sunday in school chapel.'

'Good girl. Do you think you can manage without the organ? It's a good church for singing in. Fine echo!'

'I can try!'

'Good girl!' he said again.

And it worked. He was a singer, and I was a singer, and the dark aisles and pillars of the church took us up and echoed us as if they were a whole multitude. We made the stones ring into the very far corners, where the cobwebs hung and the mice ran. There is no feeling like that.

'O Lord, open Thou our lips!'

'And our mouths shall shew forth Thy Praise!'

'O Lord, make speed to save us!'

'O Lord, make haste to help us!'

I sang like an angel, and plotted like a devil. The downfall of Mrs Brindley. I could not think what God must have thought.

We came to an end and stopped. Uncle Simon buried his face in his hands in prayer, and I pretended to do the same, but watched him through my spread fingers. He seemed to be praying an awfully long time, even for a vicar. And then I noticed that his back was heaving, as it only heaves when somebody is laughing or crying.

I knew my uncle would never laugh in church. I was left with the terrible knowledge that one of my grown-ups was crying.

And a man at that. I had sometimes seen my mother cry, though not often, and usually about the death of a beloved dog. I had never seen my father cry; though if a favourite dog had died, the muscles of his cheeks twitched very fiercely, and he chewed savagely at the ends of his grey moustache.

I walked over to Uncle Simon, cautiously. I was a little afraid, and yet I felt a power; or the beginnings of a power. I touched him on the shoulder, gently. 'Uncle?'

He raised a face wet with tears, and yet twisted with shame that I should see him thus.

'It was so beautiful,' he said. 'The singing.'

I nodded, not knowing what to say.

'It seemed so right.'

I nodded again.

'It always seems right in church. Yet the moment I go outside . . .' He looked round the church, as if desperately seeking an answer. 'They are a hard-hearted people. They have hardened their hearts against me . . .'

'There *are* some good people,' I said. Thinking of Bobbie with the cat, and his Nana looking after the whole family.

'How can *you* know, child? You haven't been among them!'

Suddenly his eyes were very sharp, even through their tears. I had nearly fallen into a snare. But I said quickly, 'There are good people everywhere.'

'True,' he said. 'Out of the mouths of babes and sucklings . . . Then it is my fault . . . Some did smile at me when I first came. There were people came to church, then . . .'

I took a deep breath and said, 'I don't think it's your fault.'

His eyes clung to mine, like a drowning man clings to a straw.

'*She* turns people away. From the vicarage door.'

Again, his eyes went sharper. 'How do you know that, child?'

'She turned me away. She didn't know who I was, but she turned me away. She didn't even ask what I wanted. I could have been someone whose mother was dying or *anything*.'

'She apologized for that; she had something in the oven and was afraid it was going to burn. You mustn't make mountains out of molehills, Caroline. But,' he got up, 'thank you for bearing with me. I feel better now.' And the vagueness came back over his eyes, and

I knew my chance was gone.

For the moment.

I knew she was looking for an opportunity to spy on me; so the next morning I gave it to her. For the cat's sake, the sooner it was over, the better. I laid a trap for her; I went out on a morning when even I might have lurked indoors, a morning with a steel-grey sky and biting wind. It was two days to Christmas.

I had a cold hour of it, crouching in the rhododendron bushes that overlooked the back door. I think I must have turned blue with cold; I almost despaired.

And then I saw the back door cautiously open, and her head come out, and look left and right. Then the whole bulk of her was tiptoeing in among the trees. It was ridiculous, the care she took; and yet she was so clumsy she made more noise than a herd of elephants. At least, in future, I knew what kind of noise to listen for.

What games I had with her; following her ten yards behind, mimicking her rolling waddling gait, until I had to stuff my hanky in my mouth to stop myself giggling out loud. (Like any fool, she never looked *behind*.) I picked up pine cones and threw them to left and right, making her jump with the small rustlings and crashes. Oh, such a game. And then, when she was at the far end of the garden from the stable, and bent almost double to peer under a monkey puzzle tree, with her great rump in the air, I crept across the silent pine needles and poked her in the burn and shouted loudly, 'Boo!'

She jumped a foot in the air; whirled with her hand at her throat, as if she was about to have a heart attack.

'Oh, Miss Caroline,' she blustered, when she got her breath back. 'You gave me such a turn.'

'Were you looking for me?' I asked mock-sweetly. 'Was there something you wanted?'

'I just wanted to know if you could do wi' a hot drink. It's such a parky morning.'

'That's very sweet of you.'

She smirked. Then I added, 'I've been following you for ten minutes. You were trying to spy on me.'

All pretence of sweetness fled. She gave me such a look of hatred that even I recoiled. I suppose even stupid people hate being caught out in their stupidity.

'You're up to some game, Miss,' she said, 'and I'll find you out. I know what you're up to.'

'And I know what you're up to.' I said.

'What *do* you mean?' She drew herself up to a great height, though her little piggy eyes flickered.

'I know what you get up to at the corner shop. Buying too much.' I suppose I meant to *really* frighten her; to frighten her away from me altogether. Blackmail, I suppose.

But it didn't work. If she'd hated me before, she only hated me more now. Some people are so stupid they have no sense of their own good at all.

'You think you're so *clever*,' she spat. 'But I'll settle your hash, missie, you see if I don't.' And then she stalked off back to the house.

I knew she would never spy on me in the garden again. What I didn't grasp was that the garden was my territory, where I had the advantage. The house was hers.

I slid carefully into the harness-room. The gentle smell of burning paraffin told me Bobbie was there. There was a second object burning paraffin now; an incredibly battered old hurricane lamp hung from a long nail, casting a soft yellow light.

Bobbie was kneeling on the floor, beside the cardboard box. He looked up, his grin enormous, his blue eyes shining as they had never done before. It might have been Christmas morning.

'They've come,' he said. 'They've come. Three of them.'

'Who?' I asked stupidly, still full of the bitterness of my quarrel.

'The *kittens*. I watched them being born. An hour ago. They came in little shiny sacks, like cellophane, on the end of little strings. She chewed them out of the sacks. I was so scared. I thought she was eatin' them. Then she licked them dry, all over. And now they're feedin off her. All purrin' their heads off. I wish you'd been here. It was marvellous.'

I suppose it should have taught me a lesson. I'd been so busy feeding my hate that I'd missed all the glory. Though of course I had seen puppies born, and I don't suppose kittens are much different . . .

'Come and see.' His voice was low and reverent, as if he was in church. And there they lay, on the hay, between their mother's outstretched legs. Climbing and pummelling with their tiny paws and treading in each other's faces; and sucking and purring at the same time like tiny bees. One all black one, one nearly all white, with black spots, and one ginger and black.

'I think I know the dad,' said Bobbie. 'Mrs Haggerty's ginger tom. He's a crafty old sod.' He picked one up, and showed it to me, cupping it ever so gently in the palm of his hands. It was the little ginger one. Its ears were crumpled like rose petals, its eyes bulged blindly behind closed slits.

Its ginger paws flailed frantic and blind, clawing the air to find a mother who had inexplicably vanished, and it squeaked piteously.

I had never seen anything so vulnerable; to come into this cruel hard world. My heart was a torrent of love. I vowed I would do murder to save it.

'Put it back,' I cried. 'Give it back to its mother. It'll catch a chill.' It was *unbearable*.

He laughed, not unkindly. 'Don't you worry; it's a tough little sod. See how it kicks!' Then he saw the look on my face, and put it back. Quickly, it snuggled back in between its siblings, and all was purring and sucking again.

'Got anything to eat?' he asked. 'The mother's ravenous. I managed to nick some bacon-rind from me dad's tea, but it was gone in a flash. Like feeding an elephant strawberries.'

I got out my little bag of scraps, and offered them to the mother. She sniffed at them, then stirred uneasily, torn between the food and the kittens. I put the bits on the hay beside her and she got upright, the protesting kittens still trying to cling to her belly, then falling away, and squealing loudly. She ate; she was wolfish, and yet with every bite, her ears swivelled to the kittens' protests. She was so frantic, my heart went out to her, too.

When she had finished, and all the uproar was over, and the kittens and cat settled in a purring mass again. I said,

'You'd better start buying her food. I can't smuggle out enough for her.'

'That's O.K. I found out when the cat's meat man comes round with his barrow. I'll meet him down the town, where nobody will recognize me.' I grinned at him. He had to act like a spy too, now. He had nosy grown-ups to dodge as well. I thought he'd make a good spy.

Then I got up. I was very tense. On the one hand were the helpless kittens; on the other, the prowling hating Mrs Brindley. She would still be watching for me, out of the house windows ...

'See you tomorrow,' I said.

'Same time, eh?' he grinned. 'I'll bring a bottle of water too. She's thirsty.'

'Milk would be better ...'

'I'll get a gill o' milk. Me Nana's got a little chipped jug she won't miss for a bit ...'

I think I fell in love with him then. With his toughness and reliability.

Oh, yes, granddaughter. You can fall in love when you're not quite twelve. With the most unsuitable people.

One day to Christmas.

It was at breakfast that disaster struck. I suppose I was too eager to nick the scraps off the plates. My uncle had left a fine big piece of ham fat on the edge of his, and had pushed it idly across the breakfast-table towards me, lost in his book. I thought I was safe. I could have pinched the tablecloth itself, when he was lost in his book. He would merely have lifted his elbows to let me take it ...

But I didn't hear Mrs Brindley come in through the door to clear up. She might have been noisy in the garden, but in the house she could move as silently as a mouse, in her old carpet-slippers. Too late, I heard the soft creak of her corset stays, and then she cried loudly.

'What are you doing with that ham fat, Miss? Don't we feed you well enough?'

My uncle looked up, bewildered, to see the large lump of ham fat in my hand.

'She was going to slip it into her cardigan pocket, sir. Look, the edge of her pocket's all greasy . . . what's this, then?' She plunged her great paw into my pocket, and flourished my bag of scraps in triumph under my poor uncle's nose.

'Caroline?' he said.

'She's a-feeding something, sir. Stealing food to feed something. I know her little ways.'

'*Are* you feeding something, Caroline?' asked my uncle, with mild interest.

God, my mind was in a whirl. Could I pretend I was feeding some poor stray dog, that came to the gate? But the gate was always shut. Could I pretend I was indeed half-starved? But I had left a lump of bread and butter on my side plate . . .

'Caroline, *please* give me an answer,' said my uncle, starting to get a little cross, while Mrs Brindley breathed heavily through her mouth in triumphant righteousness.

Then a vision of our garden at home came to my rescue in a nick of time.

'Tits,' I said.

'I beg your pardon?' said my uncle, very shocked.

I had a ridiculous desire to giggle at his pious, shocked face. But I controlled myself, and said, with an effort, 'Blue-tits, great-tits, coal-tits. They love fat. And it's the winter, and they're so *hungry* . . .'

My uncle's face cleared. 'There's nothing to be ashamed of in that. St Francis preached to the birds, Mrs Brindley. If we can't feed our feathered friends in winter . . . But there was no need to be underhand,

Caroline. If you'd asked, I'm sure Mrs Brindley would have found you lots of bits for the birds.'

'Ain't no birds in this garden, sir. I've looked many a time. She's feedin' something a lot bigger than a bird . . .'

My uncle looked torn both ways. In a moment, Mrs Brindley was going to win. A vision of the cat and kittens swam up in front of my eyes. Living. Dead. Drowned. Mrs Brindley would certainly know a man prepared to drown them; if she didn't take satisfaction in drowning them herself.

'Come and see,' I said. 'They come for me every morning. Down by the gate.' I said the gate, because the only birds I had ever seen in North Shields were sparrows, pecking their breakfasts in the mats of flattened horse-dung on the roads. But a sparrow was better than nothing . . .

We all trooped down. It would have looked ridiculous, if it hadn't been a matter of life and death. I scattered the pieces, the precious pieces, on the weedy drive, and we retired to a distance and waited.

Nothing came. We got very cold. My uncle began to fidget. Mrs Brindley's stertorious breathing got more and more triumphant. While I humbly prayed. Anything with wings, please God. Pigeons, vultures . . . Anything at all.

'Nothing,' said Mrs Brindley, at last. 'I told you, sir. No birds in . . .'

And at that moment, a solitary starling, black as soot with the smoke of the town, fluttered down. Then two more, then two more. A whole crowd, as starlings do. *Blessed* starlings; blessed, dirty starlings.

'There,' I said, when they had finished the scraps and flown away again.

'I'm not sure they're t . . . blue-tits,' said my uncle doubtfully. 'But I was never one for nature-study. However, if you *ask* Mrs Brindley, Caroline, I'm sure she will lay on plenty of scraps for you in the future.'

He walked off back to his study, leaving us glaring at each other.

I knew I mustn't go to the stables any more. Our margin of safety was now as thin as paper.

CHAPTER 5

Double Visions

All I could do was wander round the other bits of the garden disconsolately. I knew Bobbie would twig something was wrong eventually.

I was right. After two weary hours, a pine cone hit me on the ear. It was very welcome.

We hid deep in the rhododendrons, while I told him what had happened. He considered carefully. Then he said, 'She's only watching you. She doesn't know about me, right? So I can keep on feeding the cat. She's all right — I got a huge load off the cat-meat man for a penny. She ate the lot. She's got milk, too.'

'Bless you. But Brindlebags mustn't see you ...'

'She won't. I can get over the wall, right next to the stables. Lots of bricks are loose, I can make new footholds.'

As I said, he would have made a good spy.

Then he shuffled uncomfortably. 'Can I ask you a favour? There's a little girl lives next door to us. She's got TB — consumption. She hasn't got no toys, they're that hard-up. I go in to play with her sometimes, to cheer her up. She gets that bored . . . well, I told her about the kittens coming.'

'Oh, how *could* you?' I was furious. 'It was a *secret*.'

'It's still a secret, don't you worry. She knows how to keep her mouth shut. So do her parents. And nobody talks to the vicar or Mrs Brindley — they wouldn't tell her the time o' day. We're quite safe, only . . .'

'Only *what?*'

'She wants to see the kittens.'

'NO!'

He was silent, for a long time. Then he said, 'She won't make old bones, little Shirley. Me mam doubts she'll last out the winter. Says she'll be gone by spring, like the birds.'

'But how can she see them, if she's that ill?' I was still angry with him, but I was melting, under his serious gaze.

'Her mam lets her out to play, when it's not raining.

If she's well wrapped-up. We push her about in an old push-chair. She's sort of the mascot of our gang . . .'

'But how will you get her over the wall?'

'Our gang will help. Two at the bottom of the wall, and two at the top, wi' a bit o' rope. They're strong lads. We'll manage easy. We'll wait till it starts getting dark. Nobody will see us, honest. We nick the vicar's apples off his trees in summer, and nobody ever sees us then.'

'Thanks very much! I hadn't realised you were a *criminal* gang.'

But I couldn't resist his earnestness. Or the thought of little Shirley. I would still be alive next summer.

'Do as you like,' I said. 'You won't see me for a bit. I'm going to stay indoors and annoy the Brindlebags. That'll take her mind off the stables.'

And I walked away, still in a huff. Why couldn't I belong to a gang like that?

It began to snow that afternoon. Big soft flakes whirling down past the library window, as I shivered and tried to read a boring book about Christianity and the unemployed. It was full of ideas about how Christianity could help the unemployed. Setting up soup kitchens and Christian reading rooms for the men. But that was in London. It didn't seem to be

happening in North Shields ...

I heard the front door open, and Uncle Simon come in. He looked in at the library door. He had a lot of holly and mistletoe in his arms, and looked more cheerful than usual.

'The Great Feast of Christmas is about to begin,' he said.

Then Mrs Brindley came bustling out, and began to grumble about what a bother putting up holly and mistletoe was, and had the vicar got any drawing pins, for you couldn't put up holly and mistletoe without them, and there were certainly none in the house ...

That wiped all the cheerfulness off Uncle Simon's face. We'd probably never even see the holly and mistletoe. It would probably just get pushed around the kitchen table until it withered and died. I did offer to go to the corner shop for some drawing pins, saying the corner shop sold everything . . . But Mrs Brindley just asked in a nasty voice how I knew about the corner shop, and I had to shut up. Uncle Simon wouldn't have let me out into the godless town anyway.

The next morning, the snow was lying all about, deep and crisp and even. I almost hated it. It ruled out any chance of going up to see the kittens. Footsteps that led anywhere near the stables would be fatal. I just hoped cat, kittens and Bobbie were doing all right; and annoyed Mrs Brindley by offering to help put up the holly. I could tell she was a bit baffled at my staying indoors. She kept on hinting that I should go out and make a snowman or something. But I wasn't falling for that one, and just said snow was cold nasty stuff, and I *really* hated it.

There was only one consolation. My uncle insisted that she light a fire for me in the library; whether because he'd finally realised I was cold, or merely because it was Christmas Eve, it was impossible to say. She responded with a smouldering mountain of coal dust in the grate, that never showed a flicker of flame all day, however I poked and coaxed it that sent a cloud of choking smoke across the shelves of old books, every time the wind blew a fresh flurry of flakes against the windows.

I tried to forget myself in an uplifting book, full of death-bed conversions of wicked sinners. But my eyes were constantly drawn to the windows, with their view of the roof of the distant stables. How was the cat doing? Had her supply of milk dried up with the cold? Had the kittens frozen to death? Had Bobbie managed to get food in to them? Had he brought Shirley to see them yet? Several times Mrs Brindley, coming in quietly, nearly caught me staring at the stables. Even when your father was flying jet-fighters, granddaughter, I never knew such maternal worry.

But in the end the weary day passed, and darkness fell, and it was time for my uncle's return, and tea. He bustled into the library, rosy-cheeked with the cold, and unwound his enormously long scarf; but I noticed he was too wise to take his overcoat off, and he grumbled a little about the fire. Then Mrs Brindley bustled in with the tray; my uncle had laid on muffins to mark the occasion, but she had managed to burn them all round the edges. She went across to draw the curtains against the night. Then she stopped halfway, and said, in a dreadful doom-laden voice,

'There is someone in the stables! I can see a light!'

'Nonsense,' said my uncle, a little grumpily, reaching for a muffin. 'What would anyone want in our old stables?'

'Trespassers. Hooligans. Thieves,' screeched Mrs Brindley. 'They will burn the place down.'

My uncle went to the window grudgingly; I think he only meant to shut her up. And I followed him with a sinking heart.

There was a light in the lower window of the stables, showing through the trunks of the trees. Only a dim light; but as we looked, it winked, as if someone had walked across it. I cursed Bobbie in my heart, for his stupidity.

'We must ring for the police,' screeched Mrs Brindley.

'I will see to it myself,' said my uncle, huffily. He wound on his scarf again, with a deep long-suffering sigh, and set out followed by Mrs Brindley breathing fire and thunder.

'Be silent, woman,' said my uncle, 'or they will hear you and escape.' It worked; nothing else would have silenced her. I had managed to slip between them.

Our approach was quite noiseless through the snow . . .

You may wonder why I did not cry out a warning. But that would have betrayed my own position completely, and I still hoped to help somehow . . .

The silence inside the stable was absolute as well. Perhaps Bobbie had gone; perhaps the light was only the light of the stove left burning for the cats . . .

My uncle flung wide the door.

And it was then that God played one of his little jokes. Or it may have been purely an accident. I have never, all my life, been able to separate God's little jokes from accidents, granddaughter.

The scene inside the stable was the scene of the Nativity; by the red glow of the paraffin stove, and the dim golden light of the hurricane lamp, it was ex-

actly the scene on all the Christmas cards my uncle sent out. Not just the stable, with the straw on the floor, and the disused manger. But Mary was there kneeling in the straw, with her blue-clad arms round the new baby. And the ragged, tousle-haired shepherds knelt beside her in adoration, and on her left, the three kings stood, black Balthasar, crowned and splendid in red and gold, and oriental Melchior, with his calm face and blue garb, and flaxen-haired Caspar. And behind Mary, brooding, protective, stood Joseph. And all eyes were fixed in silent worship ...

And then Mrs Brindley cried, 'Thieves, hooligans,' and the children looked up startled, and King Balthasar was simply a black boy in a red and yellow bobble hat and jumper and scarf, and Mary only Shirley, a pale little girl with huge scared blue eyes and a blue overcoat with its hood up, and St Joseph was only Bobbie, with a sack draped round his back to keep out the cold, and a rough stick in his hand, and the baby was only a startled she-cat at bay, spitting in defence of her helpless mewing kittens, who sprawled in the straw.

'Fetch the poliss,' cried Mrs Brindley.

But my uncle stood as if transfixed, with the tears running down his pale fat cheeks, and I knew he had seen with my eyes, not Mrs Brindley's.

He cried out, in agony, 'Suffer the little children to come unto me, for such is the kingdom of heaven!'

'I'll run for the poliss, Reverend!' shouted Mrs Brindley.

'Shut *up*, you stupid woman,' shouted my uncle.

'I'm not standing here listening to that kind of talk,' shouted Mrs Brindley.

'Then *go*,' shouted my uncle.

And all the children just stood, open-mouthed, wide-eyed, paralysed with amazement that such things should be.

Then my uncle was among the children, shaking them by the hand one by one, babbling strange and discordant jollities.

'You must come into the house. We shall have mince pies! Ginger ale! Jellies!' He must have been lost in some distant dream of his own happy childhood. 'Come, down to the house. You are all welcome, most welcome.'

The children were torn between acceptance and flight, at such an unlikely jovial madman.

They all looked at Bobbie. He was the leader. He thought hard, narrowing his shrewd young eyes, weighing up the situation. Then he nodded; and they all trailed after the vicar. For in that town of cold and hunger and unemployment, the promise of *anything* to eat was the kingdom of heaven.

The she-cat was busy carrying her off-spring back into their box, wise and prudent mother that she was. I saw her safe in, and doused the lights for fear of fire, and then ran to join the rest.

I found them huddled in the hall. My uncle was shouting at Mrs Brindley again. 'Bring ginger ale, Mrs Brindley! Warm the mince pies!'

'We haven't got none. You didn't ask me to get any in . . . you can't expect a hardworking house-keeper to . . .'

'Surely we have *something*? Christmas cake, seedy-cake, anything!'

'Only your dinner tomorrow . . .'

'We *must* have something . . .'

'Don't talk to me like that, Vicar. I think you've taken leave of your senses . . . I will not stay one minute longer and be shouted at like that. I'm giving in my notice, as of now.'

And good as her word, she took her coat off the hook on the back of the kitchen door, and swept away without another word, slamming the front door be-hind her.

I never heard a sweeter sound. But there was a sudden horrible silence, in which hope faded from the children's faces as the real world returned, and visions

of Christmas plenty died. And my poor uncle, flapped his hands helplessly, saying over and over again,

'What shall I do? What *shall* I do? What shall I do now?'

Mrs Brindley might still have won then. But Bobbie seized his chance. He stepped forward, and stood to attention before my uncle, like a soldier.

'I can get them for you, sir! The corner shop has plenty of drink, mince pies.'

'Splendid chap,' my uncle clapped him on the shoulder, 'off you go then . . .'

Bobbie hesitated beautifully; I have never seen the late Laurence Olivier do it better.

'Oh, yes, money, money, you need money,' said my uncle fumbling up under the long skirt of his cassock and revealing a perfectly ordinary pair of dark trousers, much to the children's amazement.

He produced a very crumpled pound note. 'Here you are!' The children's eyes widened, as at all the treasures of the Spanish Main.

'Here, better have two,' said my uncle, adding another note to the first. The children looked as if paradise was assured. Bobbie and his black friend sped off like the wind.

CHAPTER 6

Merry Christmas

It was a marvellous party, all the better for being straight out of bottles, packets and tins. There should have been crumbs all over the library carpet; but these were children who pursued crumbs and picked them up with the ends of their fingers, and ate them. Afterwards, the vicar thumped away on the old piano like one possessed and we sang carols till our throats were sore. For they knew all the carols by heart, from school, even the Chinese boy, whose name I learnt was, amazingly, Ted Mulligan.

At last, when we could eat no more and sing no more, the vicar led them down to the front gate, pressing on them whatever had not already been eat-

en, for their parents and brothers and sisters. There were about thirty children by that time, for word had spread round quickly from Joe's Corner Shop that the vicar was holding a children's Christmas party, and

disbelief had been overcome by hunger, and many
had knocked on the door and been let in afterwards.

'Good night, good night,' called Uncle Simon, de-
lirious with glee. 'Merry Christmas to you all, and to

your parents.'

Now it just happened that a lot of grown-ups were passing the gate at the time, having been out to do what little Christmas shopping they could afford. I heard them muttering to each other, at the strange sight of the vicarage gate open, and happy children streaming out.

'My God, the vicar's been holding a Christmas party!'

'Wonders never cease! They'll be doubling the dole next!'

Then an adult voice called, back over its shoulder, 'Merry Christmas, Vicar!'

And all the rough adult voices were calling.

'Merry Christmas, Reverend!'

God's little joke, or the accident, was continuing.

We went back indoors, to the litter of bags and boxes and bottles on every chair and table.

'Oh dear,' said my uncle, his face suddenly falling. 'Whatever shall we do now? However can we *cope?*' He had the petulant baby look of a helpless male suddenly left to manage alone.

I knew he'd *never* manage alone. Over the days, once I was gone, the need for Mrs Brindley would come drifting back. The need to have his meals cooked, his socks darned, his shirts washed . . . inexorable. Mrs

Brindley could win yet; and extract a terrible venge-ance.

So I took a deep breath, and cut Mrs Brindley's throat for good and all. I was never sure whether that was part of God's little joke or not.

'I know a good woman who could do for you,' I said.

'A *respectable* woman?' A look of fright crossed his face.

'A respectable woman,' I said, 'and a very respectable cook. She used to work in a big house as cook, when she was younger . . .'

His eyes lit up; he was always a bit of a glutton. And I ran to Bobbie's Nana's, before he could stop me. God knows how I found the right gate in the dark. But she came, all flustered, with her hair hastily screwed up in a new bun, and a spotless white apron under her best hat and coat

He never looked back after that. At Midnight Mass that Christmas Eve, where I had expected a dreary congregation of three, we had nearly twenty. More than for years . . . word got around fast in that town. The parents of the children from the party, mainly.

And after that, with Bobbie's Nana to take him in hand, and answer his front door, and guide him with her sound common sense, his congregation grew. The next Christmas Eve, the church was nearly full; even if some of them were more than a little drunk, including my old unbuttoned friend, still grieving for his black sins.

As for Bobbie, I didn't see him again for years, after that second Christmas Eve. But I heard about his progress from my uncle. How his father got new work, as the Second World War drew nearer; building destroyers to sink U-boats. So that they could afford to send Bobbie to grammar school after all. How he was top of his class, and got all his exams. How he joined the RAF.

But it was not until 1945, April 1945, that he came walking up our drive one fine evening, when I happened to be on leave from the Wrens. He was wearing the wings of a navigator, and his left arm was in a black silk sling, and I'm afraid I didn't recognize him at first. He had grown into a very attractive young man. Not good-looking, but snub-nosed still, with warm blue eyes, and a wicked grin.

'Why didn't you look us up earlier,' I cried.

'Not till I'd done something worthwhile,' he grinned.

'Like getting yourself nearly killed?'

'And I'm still only a flight-sergeant, and you're a flipping officer . . .'

It was as if I had just left him yesterday.

'Are you going to take me out to dinner?' I asked. I was always very forward, granddaughter.

'I haven't been to university yet,' he said grimly, almost to himself.

'Oh, I can't wait till you get your degree,' I said.

And we took it on from there.

Look at him now, weeding that rockery. You've guessed, haven't you, the famous Bobbie. Grey as a badger now, though it suits him. And he's still got his snub nose and wicked grin ...

You wouldn't be here, if I hadn't been hit on the ear by a pine cone, in that horrible dark vicarage garden, all those years ago.

The cats? That vicarage was always famous for its cats. That's one of their descendants, asleep in that chair.

Beware of pine cones, granddaughter.

THE CHRISTMAS CAT

90

The
Christmas
Ghost

For my friend, Val Bierman
Thanks for all the haggis

CHAPTER I

Christmas Eve

My grownups were such marvellous *pretenders*. The way my own grandmother would solemnly help me send messages to Santa, in the dark nights before Christmas. Sitting snug by her kitchen range, I would scrawl requests on strips she tore from the edges of our local newspaper. Then she would hold them over the glowing coals, let go, and they would fly up the sooty chimney like swift singed birds.

And then there was the way, last thing on Christmas Eve, that my mother would reverently set out a clean white cloth on the kitchen table, and put on it, for Santa, a brimming glass of port wine and a freshly baked mince pie. And in the morning, early, I would find the glass empty, with big thumbprints on it. Evidence, Sherlock Holmes, evidence! I would preserve the thumb-marked glass for days, like a holy relic.

And of course, as Christmas grew near, I would be seized with an expectation so great that I could hardly sit down long enough to eat my meals. It wasn't the presents themselves, though I liked them well enough. It was the fact that he was coming. That out there somewhere in the snowy dark was this utterly powerful being who knew all about me, and whether I'd been a good boy all year, and who meant to reward me with incredible gifts. I wonder I didn't get him mixed up with God. But Santa seemed more like God's kinder, merrier younger brother, who you might dare to speak to, if you were lucky enough to catch him on his rounds.

Of course, I had doubts. The size of box my clockwork train set had come in the previous Christmas made me wonder how Santa coped with just the lads in our street, let alone all the lads in the whole world. But I just thought that Santa was an expert, with hidden tricks of his own I couldn't begin to guess at. Just like my father, who was foreman-fitter at the chemical works, and who made me things at work, like a two-foot wooden model battle cruiser, or a full size machine gun on its own tripod. With a father like mine, I had no difficulty believing there were wizards in the world . . .

Anyway, by Christmas Eve, I would be prowling non-stop, like a tiger in its cage. My mother coped by sending me on errands. She seemed to have forgotten so many items, when normally she forgot nothing. A packet of icing sugar, half a pound of currants, tissue paper, string. Every one necessitating a journey. But I didn't mind. The dark green winter sky showed off our glowing snowbound town like black velvet showed off the diamond necklaces in the jeweller's. Barrows lined every pavement, their flaring acetylene lamps illuminating landscapes of things never seen at other times. The banked sleekness of chestnuts, the silver globes of wrapped tangerines, pink exotic pomegranates and coconuts with faces like shrivelled monkeys.

And the butchers, with their rows of birds hanging like dead, plump, naked chorus girls, with just a frill of feathers at their neck, and their last agony only showing in the clenching of their feet.

And the shoppers, pirouetting like living Christmas trees, so laden with parcels as they turned and turned, calling their greetings as they passed each other.

'Aall-the-best-hinny-how's-your-Ernie—good-

can't-stop-now-Aah've-still-got-so-much-to-do-and-
he's-on-the-six-till-two-shift-so-Aaah'm-doing-it-
all-myself-this-year.' Such glad exhaustion, jubilant
desperation ...

Only in the dark background, unflustered, unhur-
ried, without hope, the unemployed men, squatting

silent on their haunches, spat into the gutter with the accurate hate of a German sniper on the Somme. I turned my eyes away from them, as I always ran past the gate of the fever hospital with my mouth shut, holding my breath. Bad luck was infectious too.

Such was my morning. After a gobbled lunch,

there were the rituals to witness. The icing of the cake and the sticking upon it of the little robin redbreast with tiny springs in place of legs, so that if you flicked him in passing, he rocked for ages. (I flicked him too hard one year, and he flew across the room and I got a clout, though not a hard one.)

Then the lettering on the mirror over the fireplace, in whitewash:

MERRY CHRISTMAS TO ALL

My mother, once a fruiterer's assistant, paints with the same elegant script in which she once announced on the fruiterer's window:

BEST COXES 6d A POUND

I am allowed to add the snowflakes; I always put on too many and my mother wipes half of them off with the hem of her apron.

Then the hanging of the decorations, my mother whimpering instructions with her mouth full of drawing pins. Then the blowing up of balloons; my lungs are very small, but my father has shown me how to do it, rubbing the balloon between my palms, and warming it at the fire. But still it usually gets away by blowing my own air back into my own lungs, or making delicious farting noises, or escaping altogether to whizz round the room like a miniature rocket, and end up sadly on the fire, and we only have six of them.

And lastly the Chinese lanterns, with their real candles, which are always hung too close to the door-lintels, so that the smell of singeing varnish is as much a Christmas smell as the aroma of my uncle's cigars.

None of these rituals will I let my mother omit, down to the tiniest detail. It is all part of the Coming of Santa . . .

And suddenly it is time for the family to be calling. And, of course, it is essential that I greet them a good two hundred yards from home, and skip wildly around them all the way, like a destroyer escorting a convoy. In fact, if they are very late, I have been known to greet them as they left their own front doors . . .

First my God-hating Aunt Rosie, basket full of newbaked mince pies, under a white cloth. I walk alongside her and reach slyly under the cloth and nick a mince pie. Still so hot it burns my mouth, while she walks along, with a tolerant smile on her face, noticing and not noticing. Tolerant of everyone, my Aunt Rose. Of everybody except God.

'Prince of Peace?' she snorts, settling herself on our couch. 'What peace? That Mussolini bombing little bairns to bits in Abyssinia? Why doesn't God strike him dead? And that poor young lass three doors down from me, four little mouths to feed an' her husband dying of TB in Preston Infirmary. What kind of Christmas is it going to be for *her?*'

For half an hour, the desolations of the world, carefully saved up for Christmas Eve, would flood our kitchen. Then she, too, suddenly brightening, would say, 'Merry Christmas, all the best, hinny!' and depart.

And then out into the dusk again, my eyes searching for the distant beloved dumpy figure of Nana, with the Christmas bird under her arm, its white unplucked feathers glinting as she passes under the street-lamp. Those feathers will soon fill the air of our kitchen, like upward-drifting snow; still cling in soft tufts to her bare brawny arms, as she reaches deep inside the bird and produces the glistening coils of pink and brown that are the mystery of the bird's inner life. And I look at the bird's face and wonder how it feels to have your insides dragged out, even if you are dead. The bird's eyes are tight shut; it looks patient and bored stiff and trying not to notice.

Nana likes to make a drama of it. 'That's the gall bladder,' she points out with gusto. 'If that bursts afore you get it out, the whole bird's ruined.' And she gives the greeny oval object an extra-dangerous squeeze for good measure, poised over the gaping belly, before dropping it safely in the bin.

Once she tried holding a white feather to my nose, as if threatening me. I must have simply looked puzzled.

'You're not like your dad then?' she said at last, very disappointed. 'Your dad was terrified of feathers when he was a bairn. He was so scared of a feather he used to wet himself.'

I couldn't believe that my dad, who was afraid of nothing, could ever be scared of a little white feather. I didn't believe her, and said so. When my father got home, she held a feather under his nose, and he stirred backwards uneasily, saying, 'Give over, Mother!'

Today, though, she is again disappointed.

'Isn't he in?'

'He's on the two till ten shift.'

'That's what Aah thowt. Only I Aah saw his bait there, with his teamakings . . .'

'Oh, dear, he's forgotten them . . .'

They both look at me. I am delighted. Another errand. The best errand in the world. My father is an oily wizard, and I am going to see him in his enchanted kingdom.

'Run along, chick,' says my grandmother. 'He'll be gasping for his brew o' tea.'

CHAPTER 2

Otto's Kingdom

Off I run. In one hand his sandwiches, knotted in their huge red spotted handkerchief. In the other, his blue enamel tea can, with its curious hedge-hog-ball of condensed milk, sugar and dry black tea leaves, to which he will add a scalding jet of water, from one of his great glowing hissing boilers.

In the dusk, the shopping crowds are thinning, but still exultant.

'Give Tommy me best!'

'See you Boxing Day!'

In a side street, church carol singers are singing "It came upon a midnight clear". One year, when I was little, they came and sang at our house, after I'd fallen asleep. I wakened, thinking they were the angels; full of joy to know the Christmas angels really existed.

But my mind was elsewhere now; on the great works of the Empire Chemical Company that filled the western horizon of the town, decorating the last of the red sunset with a hundred long plumes of smoke and steam, black, grey, blue, even red where the upward glow from an open furnace suddenly lit them.

Of course, nobody ever called it the Empire Chemical Company. Everybody called it Otto's. Otto had started it, sixty years ago. In our lads' minds, he still stalked the town. Great huge dark Otto, with his broadbrimmed hat and his beard dangling halfway down his chest. It was a good joke to borrow your dad's trilby hat, and grab your mam's smallest doormat and hold it under your chin, and run at your mates booming, 'Otto, Otto!' Otto Liebner, Otto the Jew, fabulous monster. People hated him when he first came, to make soda lime and soda ash. They thought he would use the Leblanc Process, which filled the air with green acid fumes and killed the grass and trees for miles around. People thought they were going to be choked to death in their own beds. They gave him a rough time. The kids threw dog turds at him. The men at the railway station made sure that the spare parts he ordered got lost. Then a boiler blew up and boiled three men alive. They said after that that Otto was unable to sleep; he walked the works night and day, a demon in a nightmare. To get the men to stay at their work, after their mates died, he dozed in the very place of disaster, nodding off in his huge caped greatcoat.

And then it all came right. His process, the Solvay Process, was clean and killed nothing. No more boilers blew up. After three years, Otto pronounced, 'We are not making soda ash, we are making gold!'

After that, he couldn't do enough for the town. He was the first to give the workers a fortnight's paid holiday. Public library, public baths, mechanics' institute, co-op store, new buildings for the grammar school I hoped to go to soon, all were Otto's.

A man of the people, my father said. Walked round the works all day, didn't lurk in any old office. Any worker could say anything he liked to him. But he'd felled three at once, when they got too stroppy . . .

And then he got old, so that in his great house, he had to have a lift built to take him upstairs . . . and now he was a dead hero, buried in London. But Otto's town still prospered, even in the Great Depression. Some might be out of work, but not so many as in

Sunderland, or Jarrow.

The works were still deadly, mind. Men still got killed, if they were careless. Boiled or roasted or fried. My dad had once to dismantle a coke crusher, to get a body out. He said the man's shoulders had jammed the machine, but his head was gone. That was all he ever said, except the man had been a heavy drinker, even at work . . .

So now I was heading for Otto's kingdom, which was also my father's. Past the twelve-foot wall, with glass set in the top to keep the fools out. Up to the gate, and the timekeeper's office.

I hated the timekeeper. He was not a proper man; he never got his hands dirty, my father said. What was more, he was bossy. If he saw me coming, he would grab me into his office and summon my father by phone, turning a little handle with petty vigour. He would drag my father from his work; which my father hated. And he would keep me out of the works, which I hated.

I peeped round the corner at him. He sat lounging at his long counter in waistcoat and shirtsleeves, with his flashy brass armbands to keep his cuffs high on his wrists and clean. Dark curly hair, and a little dark moustache on his pudgy face. Reading the evening paper. Call that a job, reading the paper, when my fa-

ther was risking his neck, high on the gantries, like a proper man?

I bent double, and tiptoed across the cast-iron weighbridge that lay in front of his office. I was nearly there when my tea can clanked on the iron. He jumped out of his doze, and shouted, 'Hey.'

But I was flying off into the works, where he daren't follow me. He dared not leave his little office.

Through the dusk I ran. Up the cobbled streets on which lay great lakes of water, swirling with the slick exciting patterns of oil and petrol. I skipped between them, running up thin isthmuses of cobbles, leaping from island to island to keep my best Christmas Eve shoes clean. Breathing in great lungfuls of benzol, and the lovely choky gas from the coke, that made your lungs fizz and your head spin. Rats ran from me, squeaking into corners. Pipes stuck out of walls all over the place, puffing out little clouds of green gas with a chuffing noise, or dribbling strange thick fluids

like a kid with a snotty nose. In places, the very brick-work was rotting, as patches of white or blue or green climbed up into it from out of the ground.

There was hidden life everywhere. The ground vibrated under my leather soles, to the thump of the crushers. High up among the girders, a little siren wailed, and someone clanged a huge steel door in re-

ply, and there was the terrifying avalanche rumble of falling stone, banging into metal.

Every open door showed me a scene. A black smith with the clenched face of a fiend in the glow of his furnace, beating fat pink sparks from a lump of white glowing metal. The stables where the carthorses lived; huge movement in the dark; a slow chomping;

the clink of a horseshoe, as a horse changed its weight from one leg to another; the sweet smell of hay and oats, and the lovely sweaty smell of dusty horse and rancid horse pee.

I put down my things for a moment on the windowsill, and nipped inside to have a word with old Maisie, old Ruby. Oh, the pebbly cold sweetness of a horse's nose, the huge mystery, in the gloom, of a dark shining horse's eye!

Then up with my things again and on, into the wondrous depths of Otto's kingdom, my father's kingdom, my kingdom . . .

'Yes, son? What you want?'

A man in overalls, blackened face, shining teeth and eyes. A proper man, one of my father's mates, a friend.

'Oh,' he said, 'it's Jack's lad, isn't it?' And my heart swelled with pride, at being Jack's lad.

'Let's find him then!'

And we went from man to man. 'Jack's lad's here. With his bait. Know where Jack is?'

Shouts echoing through the din.

'Think he's up number two crusher!'

'He was here, but he's gone down the bagging plant!'

'Try the limestone tower. Number three!'

My father is everywhere and nowhere, like God. Keeping the whole world running, as he would say, smooth as a Swiss watch.

We reached the base of the incredible soaring limestone tower. The figure with the black face turned to me.

'Have to leave you here. Know your way?'

CHAPTER 3

The Lift

Oh, what it is to be trusted! Up all those endless iron stairs, which had holes in their treads so that you saw the ground below, moving beneath your feet in the most lovely and terrifying way . . .

'You'd better use the lift . . . it's down . . . look, there, with the little light inside it.'

I gasped; the ultimate privilege. For this was Otto's lift.

Waste not, want not was the motto in those days.

As soon as he was dead and didn't need it any more, it was ripped out of his great house and installed in the limestone tower to save the workers' legs.

All the kids round the town said it was haunted. My father said that was rubbish. It was just that it was a funny place to put it, 'cos it was all grand and rich and fancy, in that gaunt and rusty place.

Anyway, there was no arguing. The man pushed me in and closed the doors behind me and I pushed the button, polished bright by so many thumbs, and the lift started to grind slowly and uncertainly upwards, like it was ill and dying itself.

I stood and stared around me. It was certainly the most odd thing to find in such a place. It was of the most beautiful red mahogany, still polished up near the ceiling (though very dusty) but scarred and worn by men's boots and bodies further down. The plaster ceiling was all encrusted with leaves and flowers, but cracked and brown with fumes and fag smoke. And there were mirrors set all around, in the top half of the walls. But not ordinary mirrors; they had bevel-led edges, and were cut, again, with the most intricate whirling patterns of flowers and leaves, so you could hardly see your face in them at all. I tried pulling faces at myself, moving my head around so the patterns in the glass cut my head into funny shapes. Then I got

tired of that, and wrote my name in the dust on the mahogany. Then rubbed it out quickly again, in case my father saw it.

The floor had been pretty floral tiles, but they were half worn away as well, and covered with footprints in dried grey mud. And a seat ran all round the lift, of dark red plush but threadbare and oilstained now, except in the corners. I thought it was a shame, that such a spoilt rich pretty thing should have to end its life in such a place. Like some lovely racehorse pulling a coal cart.

The lift seemed to be taking forever. It would have been quicker to climb the stairs. I just hoped it wouldn't break down and leave me stuck . . .

Then I went back to pulling faces again . . .

It was then I saw the other face, in the mirror. Behind me. It made me jump, I can tell you. All alone in that little confined space, where I thought I'd been by myself.

Then I laughed out loud. Because it was the face of Santa Claus; the fat face with the bright red cheeks, the white hair, the long, curly, snowy beard, the tiny dark eyes, half-buried in fat. Somebody must have pinned up a Christmas card, for the festive season!

I spun round to look at the card.

It wasn't there. I couldn't see anything but the

dusty mahogany walls, the patterned ceiling, the scarred floor and the worn seats of red plush.

Nothing.

Oh, c'mon I thought. There has to be a sensible explanation. It must be all these patterns cut in the mirrors that's doing it. And my imagination. I had a terrible imagination. Once I came running home crying, saying that I'd seen a poor dead cat in the street, that had been run over, and all its guts were hanging out. I mean, I hadn't dared go nearer to it than ten yards, but I'd seen its eyes and ears, and the blood. My father went out with me, for he was fond of cats. Then he began laughing and dragged me up to it, and it was nothing but a crumpled wet old jacket, that somebody had tossed down as rubbish.

So I turned back to the mirror, angling my head this way and that, trying to make it do again what it had done before. And then I found a clear two inches of mirror and ...

Got the face again. I just thought it funny that Santa wasn't wearing his red cap. Just his snowy hair ...

And then the face moved; changed its expression. It didn't turn all evil or anything. Just desperate and terrified.

Again I spun round. And there was nothing there.

Then the lift arrived at the top with a bump and a bang, and a little bell rang, and I was struggling to get that lift door open like a mad thing, with the tea tin still clutched in one hand, and the red bait-hanky in the other.

'All right, all right, hold your horses,' said a cross voice. 'What's the hurry? Where's the bloody fire?'

It was my father's voice, and that calmed me. Then he got the lift doors open from the other side, and I more or less fell into his arms.

He held me away at arm's length, and surveyed me coolly.

'Oh, you've brought me bait,' he said. 'What's the rush? Think I might starve to death?'

The men behind him laughed, but not cruelly. Just the way men will laugh at a young lad, when they're in a good humour.

Then he said (for he was no fool where I was concerned): 'What's upset ye?'

And I was so beggared to know what I should say, how I should explain, that I made a shruggy joke of it.

'Thought I saw Santa Claus in the lift.'

If I thought I would get a laugh, I was very wrong.

There was a sudden awful silence.

'What d'you mean?' asked my father sharply. 'Santa Claus in the lift?'

'Just an old bloke with white hair and a beard an' rosy cheeks. He looked a bit like Santa.'

'You mean, he came up wi' you an' got off half-way?'

'That'll only be old Sammy Dawes,' said one of the men behind him, as if anxious to close the subject. 'Only he's got a white moustache not a beard. He is a bit like Father Christmas, is old Sammy.'

'Nobody got on with me,' I said. 'And nobody got off the lift halfway. This was just a face I saw in the mirror. An old guy with rosy cheeks and white hair and beard.'

'Strewth,' said one of the men behind my father.

And another muttered a word that sounded like 'Otto.'

'Only,' I said, 'I thought he was a Christmas card somebody had pinned up on the wall. Then I saw his face move. But when I turned round, there was no-body there ...'

The silence, on top of that high tower, deepened, so that I heard the soft sighing of the breeze through the girders, and somewhere a loose piece of corrugated iron flapped and banged, making me jump.

'A white beard an' rosy cheeks,' muttered one man.

'It's him,' muttered another. 'How did he look, son?'

'Terrified,' I said. 'Desperate.'

I could tell from the look on my father's face that he was suddenly terribly angry with me. He could've hit me, though he was never the hitting sort.

'It's him,' said the first man again. 'It's old Otto.'

'Come to warn us. There's goin' to be a death in the plant tonight.'

'Don't talk so bloody wet,' snapped my father. 'That's nothing but old wives' tales.' He turned on the man who had spoken. 'Have you got nothing better to do? D'you think this plant runs itself?'

'Bloody wet, nowt!' said the man defiantly. 'Davy Nessworthy saw old Otto that night afore Billy

Stansfield fell into the crusher. In the lift. In the mirror. Didn't you, Nesser?'

'Aye, Aah did.' Davy Nessworthy was small but determined, not to be put down. He glared at my father harder than my father glared at him.

'You're worse than a pack of old women,' shouted my father. 'Get back to work, afore I sack the lot of you. And think on what you're doing, or somebody will get killed by carelessness. Keep your minds on your work.'

'You'll check up on things, Jack?' Little Nesser asked my father. 'Keep your eyes open? We don't want some woman widowed on Christmas Eve . . .'

My father looked at them. Even I could see they had the wind up, and my father knew them better than I did. He said, his voice going a bit gentler, 'I'll keep my eyes open. I'll check up on things, like I always do. Have I let you down yet? And don't go phoning every part of the works, the moment me back's turned, making them nervous. I want everybody to have a merry Christmas . . .'

They murmured again, a little placated. Then he turned to me.

'I'll see you out of the gate. You've caused me enough worry for one night.'

'Don't be hard on the lad, Jack,' said Little Nesser.

'He only said what he saw. How could he know what old Otto looked like?'

My father made a sound of exasperation deep in his throat; half a grunt and half a snarl, almost the noise men make before they spit. Then he shoved me into the lift in front of him.

I didn't see anything in the mirrors on the way down. I didn't even dare look into them, with his eye on me. I kept my own eyes on the worn, ornate footprinted tiles on the floor.

He marched me to the gate, his hand on my elbow, almost like I was under arrest. Then gave me a shove out into the night; and nodded to the dozy timekeeper.

'That your lad?' said the timekeeper, nervously. 'I thought it was him sneaking in. But he was too quick for me.'

'You're too slow to catch cold,' said my father, his anger still hovering. Then he called after me, 'Straight home, mind! Tell your mam I won't be late.'

CHAPTER 4

Black Widows

I ran off in relief that it hadn't been worse. As I said, my father wasn't a hitter; but he was a brooder. If I incurred his disgust, he sometimes wouldn't speak to me for days. A thunderstorm hung over the house. Sometimes I wished he'd hit me and get it over with.

But as I slowed to a walk, before I got a stitch in my side, I started to worry. All the things the men had said kept going round in my mind. Little Nesser was right. I hadn't known what old Otto had looked like, in the last years of his life. To me, as to all the lads, he was a huge striding figure with a big black beard. So how could I have invented the pathetic little Santa of the mirror?

And Little Nesser had seen him, the night Billy Stansfield fell into the crusher . . .

And . . . the word 'widow' kept going round and round in my mind. I knew the widows from the works. They walked round our town, always in black, never smiling, carrying some terrible burden so I sometimes crossed the road to avoid them. Their faces were so still, as if nothing was ever going to happen again in their lives except the bearing of the burden. And their kids had the same still expression; they were not normal. They were no good at school work or games. They didn't even try. And they might suddenly burst out crying without warning, horrible crying that went on and on. They were like bombs waiting to explode. You never played with them; never went calling for them at their houses. When you had to go to their back doors, on an errand for your mam, you noticed their houses smelt funny. We all thought it was the smell of death . . .

Somewhere in the town there was some ordinary woman, busy getting ready for Christmas, humming carols, tying up presents, getting the bird stuffed, all happy . . .

Who would be a widow by morning.

For the rest of her life.

I thought about God, waiting and watching and letting it happen. Sitting up there above the clouds, listening to all the carols being sung in his praise, sending out the angels to Bethlehem to proclaim tidings of great joy to men of goodwill, and letting some poor beggar at Otto's get himself fried to death by molten soda ash, or boiled alive in a vat of caustic till the flesh came off his bones like the Christmas turkey's.

I knew there was no point to praying about it, like I used to pray about passing my exams, or being bullied by David Black. God did do small favours. But my aunt was right. He wouldn't do anything about this. It was his business, not my business.

And it was no good asking Santa. All that poor silly sod could do was go on giving out presents; so some kid would get presents and a boiled-alive dad. And my father would do his best, would check everything like he always did. But he hadn't been able to stop Gordon Stansfield's dad falling into the crusher . . .

And then the terrible thought struck me that it might be my dad who copped it. He might be foreman, but that wouldn't save him if some pipe burst and the steam shot out. In fact he'd be in more danger than all the rest, because he would prowl around till the end of his shift looking for the cause of trouble, walking into danger. Like a man stalking a tiger.

And then my mam would be a widow and wear black and walk round with a still, frozen face for the rest of her life. And I would turn rotten at school work and sport, and nobody would want to play with me any more . . .

I turned a corner, and walked into the middle of the Sally Army. They had given up promising Hell to drunkards for one night in the year, and were playing "Once in Royal David's city . . ."

I nearly threw up in the gutter there and then. The thought of the comfort of home, the curtains drawn and the coal fire blazing up the chimney and the dog snoozing in front of it, and me mam happily frying sausage and chips for tea, our usual Christmas Eve treat . . . and my Nana getting the bird into the oven to roast until it was brown and crisp . . .

I couldn't go home. Home was a warm and cosy trap, with nothing to think about but worry about me dad.

I hovered on the kerb, listening to the Sally Army and staring down at a broken beer bottle in the gutter.

And then it came to me.

There was one thing that could help; there was

one thing that knew what was going to happen.

The face in the mirror.

I knew now it had been trying to tell me something. Warn me in time.

I had to go back. I had to go back and face it, and work out what it was trying to say.

God, if I got caught this time, my father would kill me. He'd skin me alive. He wouldn't speak to me for a month, and he'd think I'd done it to make a fool of him in front of the men. He might never speak to me for the rest of my life.

But I'd rather have him not speaking to me than have him in a black coffin, roasted like a Christmas turkey. At least he'd still be alive . . .

I started to run back towards the works. Then I slowed to a walk. It wouldn't do to arrive panting and shaking. The timekeeper would hear me coming a mile off.

CHAPTER 5

The Return

Everything seemed to go wrong. I decided, when I got near the gate, to take my shoes off so my steel heel and toe caps wouldn't click on the iron weighbridge. I took them off, and tied them together and hung them round my neck. Then, bent double, I started to cross and discovered too late what I should have remembered, that the weighbridge itself was studded with squares of iron an inch across, that pressed into my bare feet like torture implements. By the time I got to the far side, my feet were agony. Then I discovered that the bows I'd tied in my shoelaces had turned into knots, tight knots. I had to cower in a dark tunnel that led off to the right, trying to untie the knots in the dark. And the knots were tight, and my mam had just cut my fingernails after my Christmas bath . . .

It seemed to take me half an hour, and all the time the rats were squeaking about and running across my feet and I was scared they'd bite me with their poisonous fangs and I was expecting a crash or a bang, or a flash or a scream, and to hear the works' siren hoot out its terrible emergency hoot that told the whole town that some poor devil had copped it.

I got my shoes on again at last, and headed for the limestone tower, which seemed to fill the sky, the light of the works' street lamps staining it upwards with a dim glow.

And there seemed to be men everywhere now. They were no longer my allies. They mustn't see me, or they'd send for Dad. I seemed to have to cower in every doorway. And the men didn't just walk past now whistling, like they usually did; they gathered in groups near me, and muttered in frightened voices, and I knew what they were talking about. In spite of my father's orders, the word about Otto had got around. And I grew afraid that by spreading that word, by spreading panic, I was going to make the accident happen. When one of the men got into a tizz and made a fatal mistake. And it would be all my fault . . .

I died a thousand deaths, before I got to the foot of that tower. And then saw to my horror that the lift wasn't there. I could see it motionless, high up among the girders. I would have to wait for it to come down.

It was five minutes before I remembered you could summon lifts by pressing the button; so you can see what kind of state I was in.

It came at last. The door began to open, when I suddenly realised to my horror that there was somebody inside. And no ghost either. Two big black-faced men with jangling tea cans. It was too late to hide. If I ran, they'd chase me. So I just stood and nodded to them, as I had often seen them nod to each other.

'Thought you'd gone home,' said the bigger man, friendly enough.

'I forgot something,' I said.

'Your dad's not up there. He went to number four crusher.'

'It's Little Nesser I want,' I said, staying cool somehow.

'Mr Nessworthy to you, son,' said the bigger man severely. Then they nodded and went away. And holding my breath, I got inside the lift, closed the doors and pressed the big brass button, still kept shiny by the constant pressure of men's thumbs.

The lift began to slowly jerk upwards. And my eyes

flicked from mirror to mirror, in a mixture of desperate hope and total disbelief. I mean, it was such an odd place. I saw mirror within mirror within mirror. And all dim and entangled in the mass of cut glass, overlapping foliage of flowers and stems and leaves. I could see the front of my face and the back of my head in the same mirror. And if I looked sideways, I could see myself, a whole row of me standing like a row of soldiers standing to attention, curving away into forever . . . how could I find what I wanted to know in that endless maze?

'C'mon,' I said desperately. 'C'mon. There's not much time.' As I would to another kid.

And then suddenly, I knew he was in the lift with me.

Not in the mirrors. In the lift itself, sitting behind me. And as I turned, I shut my eyes, afraid that I would see him. And when I did see him, through near-shut eyes, a wave of shock hit me, as if I'd been standing in the shallows on a beach, and it had been an icy wave of the sea.

He sat, in the far corner. I still have the crazy impression that the seat sagged a little under his heavy bulging thighs. He looked so solid and real, you see. The slightly greasy folds of his waistcoat, with its heavy gold watch and chain. His boots, highly polished but old and cracked, as if they were a favourite pair of boots he could not bear to part with. The carnation in his buttonhole, that showed up so frighteningly fresh and young, against the dying sagging yellow of his face. The length of his white beard, stained brown with tobacco at each side of his mouth. The white hair that made him look like Santa Claus in the mirror; the rosy cheeks that I could now see were an unhealthy network of broken veins.

The lift was full of the smell of old man, like the smell of my grandfather's house. The lift was full of the sound of his breathing, as he pressed his heavy-fingered pudgy hand against his side, as if to stem some tide of pain. His mouth was open, and black inside.

But he didn't frighten me. His face was agonised; but kind. I was only scared he would die again at any moment, before my very eyes, before he could tell me what I had to know.

'Where?' I managed to gasp out. 'Where's the . . .'

He understood. His eyes looked right, towards one corner of the lift, one corner of the whole limestone tower. Then, unable to speak for his gasping, he raised both pudgy hands in the air and brought them down with a scissors movement, making a diagonal cross in the air. And then he really did begin to die,

and I couldn't bear to look.

But when I heard the lift clang home at the top I looked again. And he was gone. And the smell.

Somebody opened the lift doors, and I practically fell out, breathing in the coke-tainted air as if it was the freshest I had ever breathed.

'Where's Mr Nessworthy?' I said.

'Here, son, here.' Little Nesser came forward and grabbed me before I fell, as the high gantries rocked around me against the dark sky.

'You've seen him again?' asked Little Nesser, his sooty greasy face very close to mine.

'Aye,' I gasped. 'He showed me where the danger was. I think. He nodded *that* way.' I nodded my head in the direction of one corner. 'And he made a sign like *this*.' I feebly sketched the sign in the air, wondering if anyone would understand.

Nesser frowned. Then he said, 'The cross-stanchion! By God, the cross-stanchion. If that's going, we're all dead men.'

CHAPTER 6

Five Minutes to Midnight

It was too much for me. I must have fainted, and I was glad to faint. Except that they told me afterwards that I nearly fell through the safety-railing, and if Little Nesser hadn't grabbed me, I'd have fallen two hundred feet. But I didn't know anything of that. Only my ears were still working, as I heard someone whirling the handle on the telephone, and Little Nesser's voice yelling for my father to come. And, a bit later, I came round and saw my father being lowered over the railing on a thick rope, with a big torch in his hand. His last act was to take off his greasy old cap and hand it to one of his mates, as if it was something precious. And I watched through the holes

in the metal walkway and saw his tiny lamplit figure
dwindle and dwindle, until he landed with his feet on
a great X of concrete that made him look no bigger
than an ant. I saw him kick at the concrete with his

steel-tipped boot. And the concrete exploded and fell away in fragments out of the lamplight. And I heard Nesser say, 'He's signalling. Close the tower down. *Close her down.*'

And a bell rang, and the biggest, nearest rumbling ceased, and it almost seemed like a total silence.

Then I heard Nesser say, 'Bring him up, lads. Very slow and easy.'

Then my father climbing back over the rail, saying, savagely, 'The concrete's rotten. Rotten as dry shit. The reinforcing rods are rusted through. Get everybody out of here.'

They sent me down with the first liftful.

They sent me home in the shift-manager's car, a little Austin Seven. Everybody seemed to want to help me into it; hands kept touching me and patting me on the back or the shoulder. I hardly noticed the journey home; the houses and street lamps were just a whirl in the dark.

The driver kept on telling my mother that I'd saved lives. My mother kept on saying that she hoped I'd behaved myself and not done any harm. Then she put me to bed and brought an enamel bowl of warm water and bathed my face and hands very gently, and I complained about being put to bed early on Christ-

mas Eve.

I must have fallen asleep by the time my father got home. What woke me was the way the bed sagged, when he sat down on it; and his comforting smell of coke fumes and fag smoke, that never really left him, however often he had a bath.

'You awake?'

'Aye.'

'They've closed the whole works down. Frightened the vibration'll finish off the limestone tower. It's hanging by a bloody thread o' metal. I'd never have guessed that cross-stanchion would go. The fumes must a' rotted the concrete; it's only thirty years old . . .'

'Wasn't your fault,' I said stoutly.

'No. Aah've only got charge o' the moving parts. Civil engineer's fault, who built it. He's probably dead years ago. Feller called Chapman.'

There was a long silence then.

Then, he said, 'Lucky Little Nesser spotted it. I'll not ask what you thought you were doin' there . . .' More silence, and sounds of my father struggling with his beliefs. Finally he said, 'Otto died in that lift, you know. His heart gave out, poor old beggar.'

'I thought he died in London.'

'No, he was buried in London. But he died in that lift.'

I remembered the dying agonised face.

My father sighed, as if it was all too much.

'He never got over those first three men getting scalded. It preyed on his conscience, they say. He was never happy after, however much money he made. He was a good feller in his own way. True to his lights.' Then he added savagely, 'It's coming to something when little bits o' bairns have got to be used to put the world to rights.'

Then he got off the bed. He would say no more. Ever.

'Merry Christmas, Dad!'

He pulled out his watch, from the pocket of his coat, and squinted at it, in the dim light from the hall.

'Hold your horses. It still wants five minutes to midnight. Save it for the morning.'

And then he was gone.

Other books by

Robert Westall
Twice winner of the Carnegie Medal

A Time of Fire

**The sky split open. A sky of brilliant yellow light;
a world of noise that filled his ears like sand
at the seaside, so that afterwards there was
only total silence.**

It takes just a few seconds for the German bomber to
drop its deadly explosives and disappear into the clouds.
But those few seconds change Sonny's life for ever.
In the months that follow Sonny finds himself pursuing
his own dramatic and intensely personal confrontation
with the Germans.

'Deeply moving...Strong, uncompromising writing'
Telegraph

The Wind Eye

**Does a long-dead saint have the power
to destroy time itself?**

On the sombre coast of Northumberland a family
holiday starts off with the usual rows and bickerings.
Then, without warning, strange things start to happen.
At the holiday home is a weird boat, like a miniature
Viking ship. The locals claim it belongs to St Cuthbert
– but he died over thirteen hundred years ago. But
when the boat takes some of the family back into the
past, to a time of violence and terror, St Cuthbert is the
only one who can help them. But will he?

'A writer of rare talent'
Michael Morpurgo

The Making of Me:
A Writer's Childhood
Edited by *Lindy McKinnel*

'*Fascinating scenes from Westall's childhood, and insights into the development of a fine writer. A lovely book.*'
David Almond

'*A collection of Robert Westall's writings, allowing us a glimpse into his thoughts – on growing up on Tyneside during World War 2, on life and death and most of all, offering an insight into the imagination of a great writer*'
Valerie Bierman